LEARN TO READ

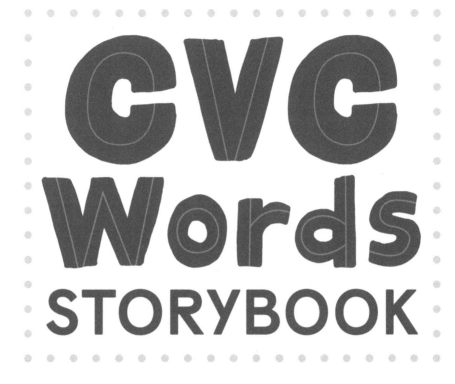

CVC Words STORYBOOK

20 Simple Stories & Activities for Beginner Readers

CRYSTAL RADKE
ILLUSTRATIONS BY CLAIRE KEAY

ROCKRIDGE PRESS

First Rockridge Press trade paperback edition 2022

Rockridge Press and the Rockridge Press logo are trademarks or registered trademarks of Callisto Media Inc. and/or its affiliates in the United States and other countries and may not be used without written permission.

For general information on our other products and services, please contact our Customer Care Department within the United States at (866) 744-2665, or outside the United States at (510) 253-0500.

Paperback ISBN: 978-1-68539-544-5 | eBook ISBN: 979-8-88608-335-4

Manufactured in the United States of America

Interior and Cover Designer: Carlos Esparza & Keirsten Geise
Art Producer: Hannah Dickerson
Editor: Elizabeth Baird
Production Editor: Ruth Sakata Corley
Production Manager: Martin Worthington

Illustrations © 2022 Claire Keay, except for the following: © Robin Boyer, pp. 6, 18, 36, 60, 66, 72, 78, 84, 96, 102, 108, 114. Pattern used under license from Shutterstock.com
Author photo courtesy of Two Toes Photography

10 9 8 7 6 5 4 3 2 1

Contents

Introduction

Welcome! I'm so glad you've chosen this book for your child. A CVC word is a single-syllable, three-letter word made up of a consonant-vowel-consonant combination. CVC words are important in early reading, as they blend together individual letter sounds, called phonemes. Children use these words when just starting to read and write because they are easy to sound out and decode.

This book includes twenty stories focusing primarily on high-frequency CVC words along with some simple sight words and, toward the end, some more advanced one- and two-syllable words. After reading each story, children can complete two activities that will help reinforce the CVC words they just learned. This book is specially designed to support your young learner and grow their confidence as they embark on their reading journey.

Please keep in mind that while stories progress from easiest to hardest, every child learns at a different pace. If you need to spend more time on a story, please do! What's most important is fostering a love of reading in every child, as it is the foundation of most learning throughout their life.

Note to Caregivers

This book is intended for beginning readers with knowledge of letters and sounds. Children will need to be able to recognize letters and know the sounds they make to decode the CVC words in this book. The beginning stories have fewer words and repetitive text, which will make it easier for children to get started. To get the most out of each learning experience, working through each story together with your child is recommended.

There are different approaches to reading each story. The adult can read the story first, the child can read the story first, or you can read it together. As the adult, you could also read the first sentence in the story and then have the child read the remaining sentences.

Set a reading goal with your child. You can read one story each day, every other day, or once a week. I suggest rereading the previous story before starting the new story to help build fluency. You can also use this extra learning opportunity to ask comprehension questions, such as "What is the story about?" and "Who is in the story?"

Be sure to read each page at the child's pace. If they are struggling, you can help them by pointing to the words as you read them and sounding out each CVC word for or with them. Then have them reread the sentence on their own. Once they finish the story, you could always have them read it again, right then or later. The important thing is that they are engaged and having fun.

After successfully reading a story, if they have lost interest or are struggling with attention, come back later to help them complete the activity pages. They can be completed all at once or one page at a time. It will be important to follow the young learner's lead; as their stamina grows, they'll be able to handle more pages in one sitting.

Happy reading!

Crystal Radke

The Cat Sat

FOCUS CVC WORDS:

cat, sat

The cat sat.

The cat sat here.

The cat sat here.

The cat sat here.

The cat sat here.

The cat got up!

LEARN TO READ: CVC WORDS STORYBOOK

Activity Time

Read the words. Then trace the words.

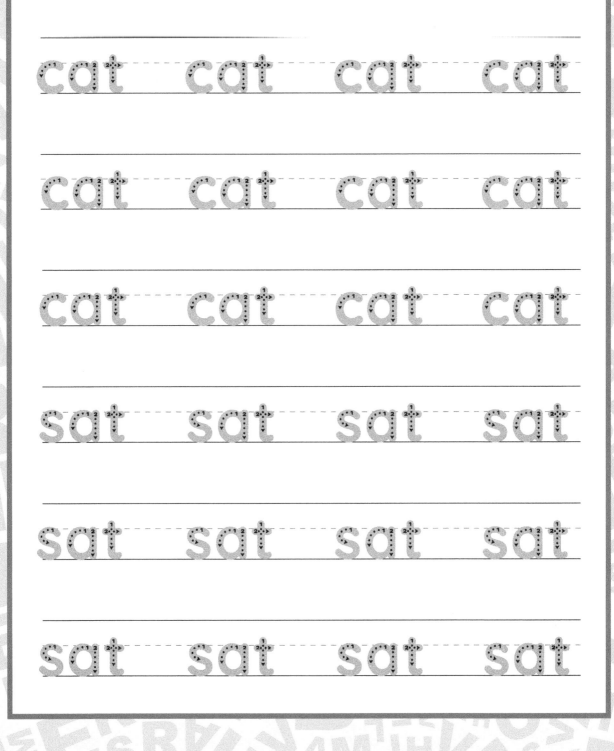

Activity Time

Color each cat that has the word **cat** or **sat**.

 cat

 van

 hen

 big

 sat

 hit

 vet

 tub

 cat

 sat

 lid

 pot

LEARN TO READ: CVC WORDS STORYBOOK

My Bag

FOCUS CVC WORDS:
had, bag

I had a bag.

I had a hat in my bag.

I had **gum in my** bag.

I had **a bat in my** bag.

I had **a cup in my** bag.

I had **a big** bag.

Activity Time

Read the words. Then trace the words.

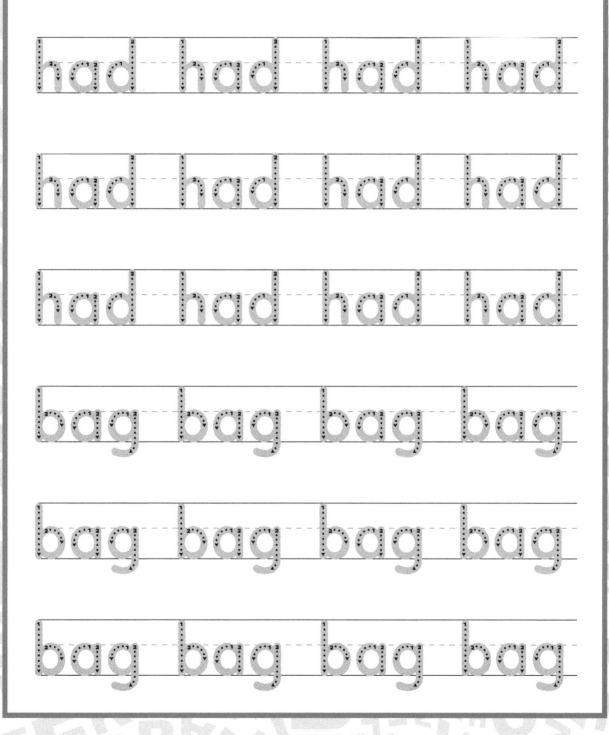

Activity Time

Find the word **had**. Draw a line under each one. Then find
the word **bag**. Circle each one.

had

big

got

cat

bag

pig

bag

sun

cub

run

dog

bag

sun

cat

cub

bag

sat

dad

fun

had

big

pig

run

sat

had

The Big Pig

FOCUS CVC WORDS:
big, pig

The **big pig** is in the pen.

The **big pig** can sit.

LEARN TO READ: CVC WORDS STORYBOOK

The big pig **can run.**

The big pig **can hop.**

The big pig is in the mud.

The big pig had fun.

LEARN TO READ: CVC WORDS STORYBOOK

Activity Time

Read the words. Then trace the words.

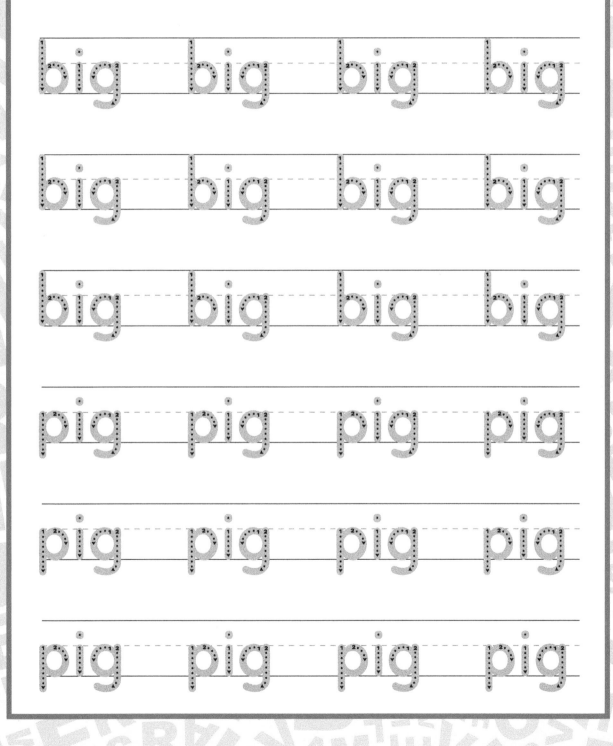

Activity Time

Color each space that has the word **pig** or **big**.

big

big

can

pig

fun   den   mop

sun

pig

pig   big

big   pig

run

dad

pig

pig   pig

LEARN TO READ: CVC WORDS STORYBOOK

My Dog Spot

FOCUS CVC WORDS:
dog, got

My dog got **big.**

My dog got **fed.**

My dog got up and ran!

My dog got wet.

My dog got **in the tub.**

My dog got **a hug.**

LEARN TO READ: CVC WORDS STORYBOOK

Activity Time

Read the words. Then trace the words.

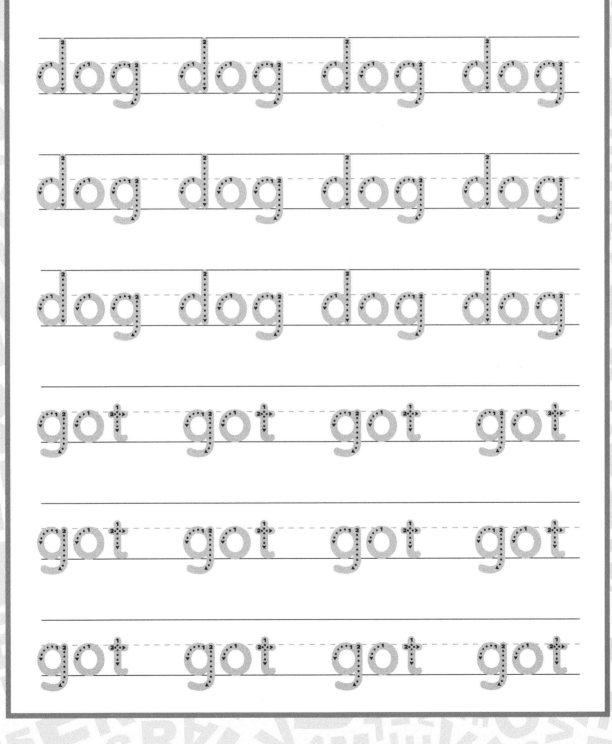

Find the word **dog**. Draw a line under each one. Then find the word **got**. Circle each one.

tub

got

hen

dog

mat

sun

mat

got

pot

dog

cat

jug

fun

mud

dog

hat

got

big

net

got

mat

sit

dog

pen

lid

It Is Wet!

FOCUS CVC WORDS:
get, wet

Is it wet yet?

Yes. Cam will get wet.

Sam will get wet.

The van will get wet.

The rat will get wet.

I will not get wet!

LEARN TO READ: CVC WORDS STORYBOOK

Activity Time

Read the words. Then trace the words.

Activity Time

Color each circle that has the word **get** or **wet**. Then follow the colored circles to complete the maze.

get	had	bag	cat	big	pig
wet	get	sat	dog	got	fun
sun	wet	dad	run	den	cub
can	get	mop	pet	vet	bet
hug	wet	pal	bed	wet	hit
big	get	wet	get	wet	get
ten	nap	hen	pen	pot	wet

Fun in the Sun

FOCUS CVC WORDS:
fun, sun

I had **fun** in the **sun**.

The man had fun in the sun.

The gal had fun in the sun.

My pal had fun in the sun.

Spot had fun in the sun.

We had fun in the sun.

LEARN TO READ: CVC WORDS STORYBOOK

Activity Time

Read the words. Then trace the words.

Color the suns that say **fun** or **sun**.

 had

 fun

 cat

 sun

 bag

 fun

 fun

 sun

 sat

 sun

 big

 dog

The Hen in the Pen

FOCUS CVC WORDS:
hen, pen

The hen is in the pen.

The hen is big and red.

LEARN TO READ: CVC WORDS STORYBOOK

The pen has mud in it.

The hen pecks in the pen.

I fed a fig to the hen in the pen.

The hen ate the fig in the pen.

LEARN TO READ: CVC WORDS STORYBOOK

Activity Time

Read the words. Then trace the words.

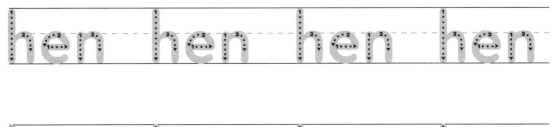

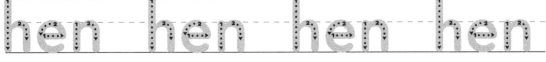

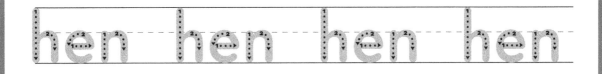

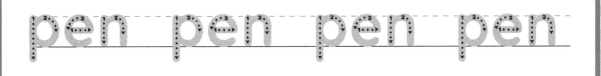

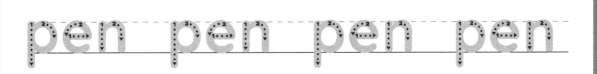

Activity Time

Find and circle the word **hen** three times. Find and circle the word **pen** three times.

h p e n l a
e o t r i h
n p o y k e
t l i p e n
u h e n z a
p e n e t p

Time to Eat

FOCUS CVC WORDS:
pot, lid

The ham is in the pot.

The pot has a lid.

The lid on the pot is big.

The lid and the pot are hot.

We take off the lid.

We take the ham from the pot. Yum!

LEARN TO READ: CVC WORDS STORYBOOK

Activity Time

Read the words. Then trace the words.

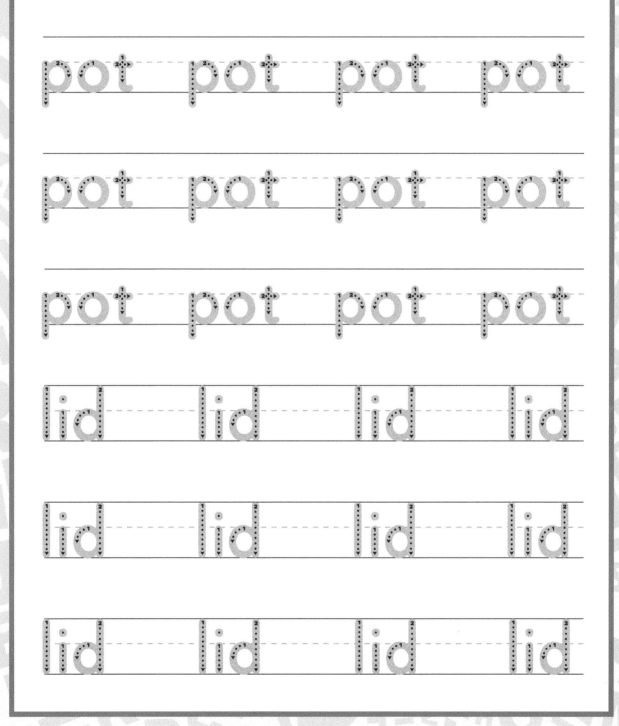

Activity Time

Color each circle that has the word **lid** or **pot**. Then follow the colored circles to complete the maze.

LEARN TO READ: CVC WORDS STORYBOOK

My Pet Is at the Vet

FOCUS CVC WORDS:
pet, vet

My pet is at the vet.

My pet ran from the vet.

LEARN TO READ: CVC WORDS STORYBOOK

The vet pats my pet.

The vet likes my pet.

My pet **likes the** vet.

My pet **did well at the** vet.

Activity Time

Read the words. Then trace the words.

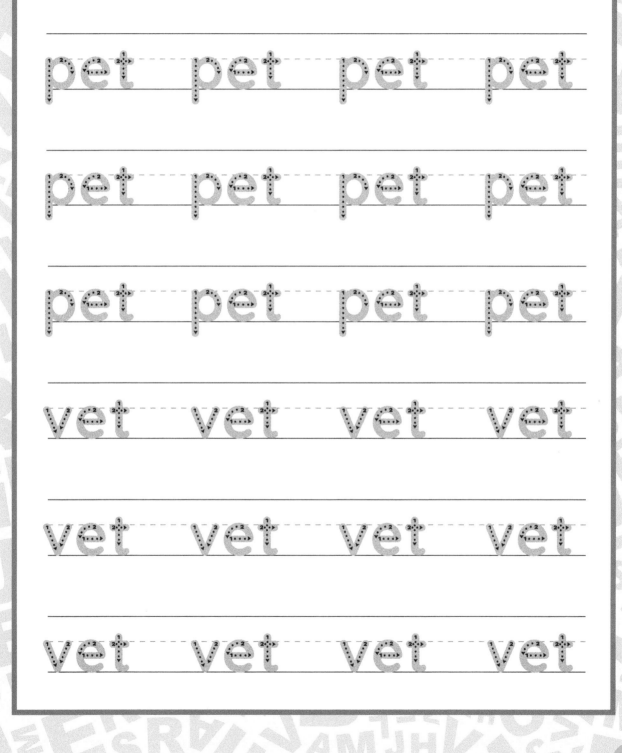

Activity Time

Find the word **pet**. Draw a line under each one. Then find the word **vet**. Circle each one.

had

bag

sat

pet

pig

cat

fun

vet

sun

dad

run

cub

den

pet

man

pet

cut

vet

pal

vet

sad

pot

pet

vet

bet

My Dad Likes to Run

FOCUS CVC WORDS:
dad, run

My dad **can** run.

My dad **can** run **in mud.**

My dad can run and run and run.

My dad can run fast.

My dad **can** run **home.**

Hi, Dad**! I can** run **to him.**

Activity Time

Read the words. Then trace the words.

Activity Time

Color the shoes that say **dad** or **run**.

 den

 dad

 dad

den

dad

can

 run

 mop

 pal

run

mop

pal

 run

 hug

 dad

run

hug

dad

The Cub in the Den

FOCUS CVC WORDS:
cub, den

The cub is in the den.

The cub has a log in the den.

The cub sits in the den.

The cub eats in the den.

The cub naps in the den.

The cub plays out of the den.

LEARN TO READ: CVC WORDS STORYBOOK

Activity Time

Read the words. Then trace the words.

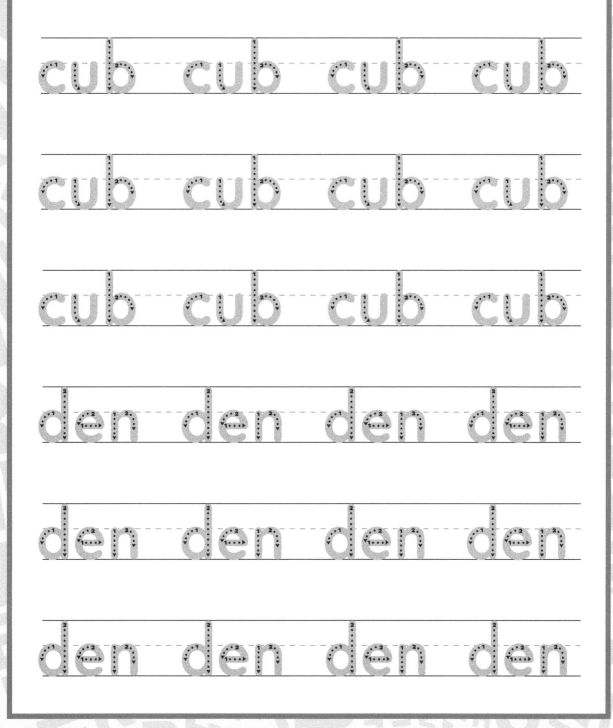

Activity Time

Write the words **cub** and **den** on the lines below. Then color the pictures.

_____

- - - - - - - - - - - - - - -

_____

_____

- - - - - - - - - - - - - - -

_____

LEARN TO READ: CVC WORDS STORYBOOK

Nap Time

FOCUS CVC WORDS:
bed, nap

It is time for a nap in my bed.

I sit on my bed to nap.

My pet dog sits by my bed.

I will nap in my bed.

My pet dog will nap by my bed.

We will take a long nap now.

Activity Time

Read the words. Then trace the words.

nap nap nap nap

nap nap nap nap

nap nap nap nap

bed bed bed bed

bed bed bed bed

bed bed bed bed

Activity Time

Write the sentence "I will nap in bed." Then color the picture and draw yourself taking a nap on the bed.

I Can Mop

FOCUS CVC WORDS:

can, mop

I can **get** the mop.

I can mop **over here.**

LEARN TO READ: CVC WORDS STORYBOOK

I can mop **over there.**

I can mop **a big spot here.**

I can mop a big spot there.

Oops! I can mop up the mess.

Activity Time

Read the words. Then trace the words.

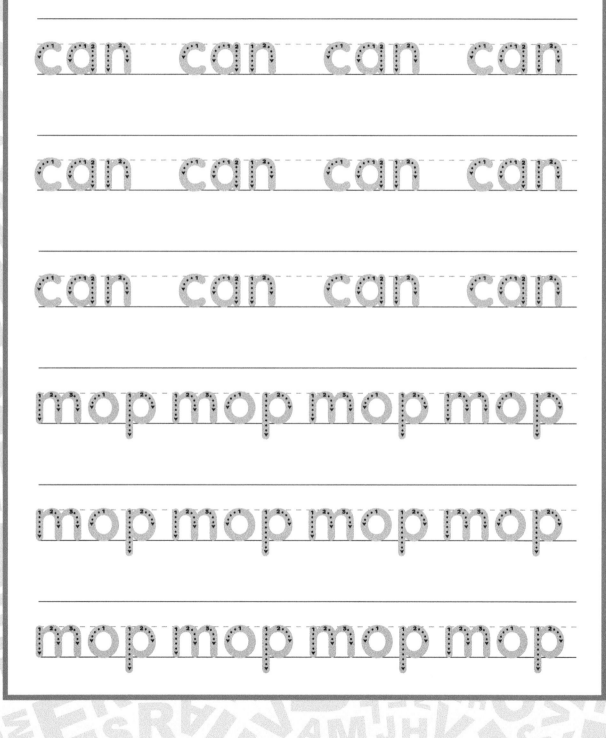

Activity Time

Color the drops with the word **can** or **mop** in them.

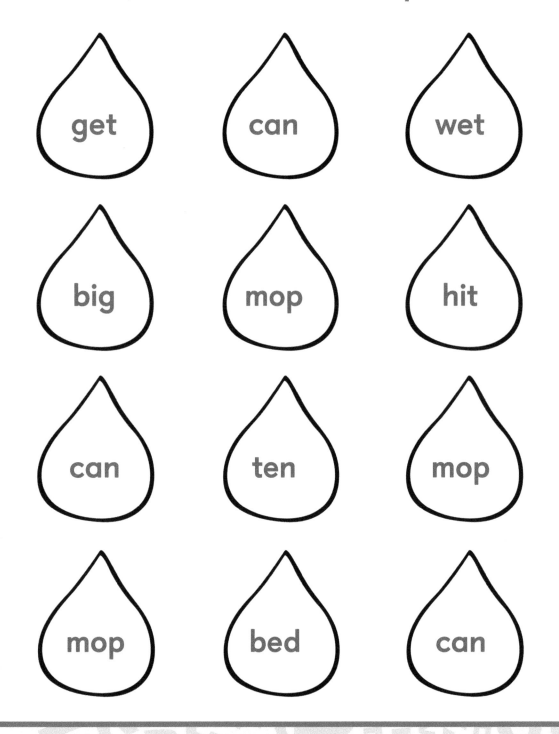

get

can

wet

big

mop

hit

can

ten

mop

mop

bed

can

My Pal Likes to Hug

FOCUS CVC WORDS:
pal, hug

My pal likes to pet and hug his dog.

My pal likes to pet and hug his cat.

My pal likes to run and hug his gram.

My pal likes to run and hug his pop.

My pal likes to sit and hug me.

My pal likes to hug a lot.

Activity Time

Read the words. Then trace the words.

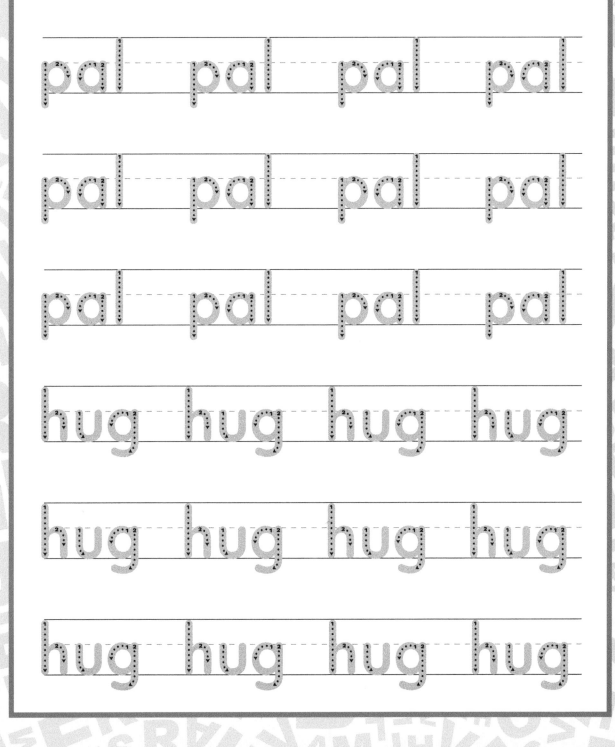

Activity Time

Color the monsters that say **pal** red. Color the monsters that say **hug** blue.

 pal

 hug

 nap

 hug

 pal

 hen

 pen

 pot

 hug

 jug

 bug

pal

LEARN TO READ: CVC WORDS STORYBOOK

Hit the Ball

FOCUS CVC WORDS:
bet, hit

I bet I can hit the ball.

I bet I can hit the ball with my bat.

I bet I can hit the ball far.

I bet I can hit the ball to him.

I bet I can hit the ball to her.

I did hit the ball far!

LEARN TO READ: CVC WORDS STORYBOOK

Activity Time

Read the words. Then trace the words.

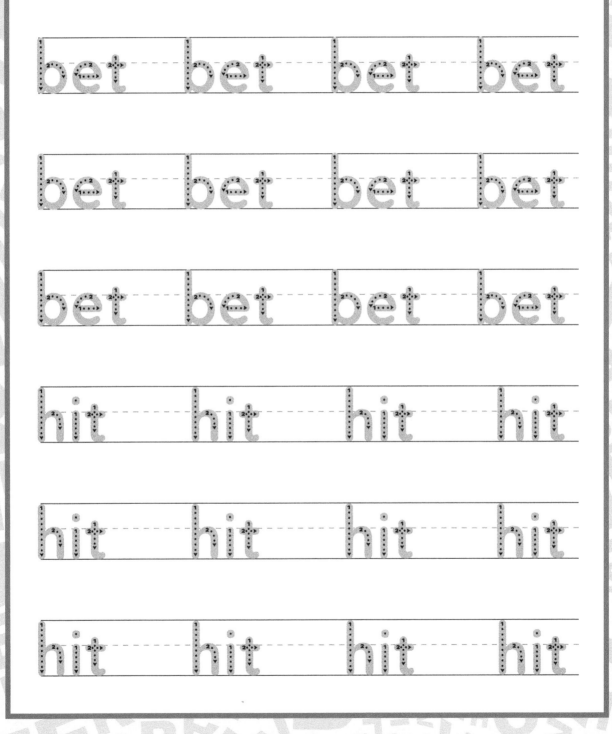

Activity Time

Color each circle that has the word **bet** or **hit**. Then follow the colored circles to complete the maze.

bet	cut	sad	mud	log	big
hit	sit	net	mat	rig	man
bet	hit	tub	cup	van	bug
jug	bet	hit	bet	hit	bet
lid	pot	pen	hen	nap	hit
bed	ten	big	lid	pot	bet
wet	get	vet	pet	hug	hit

Let's Dig

FOCUS CVC WORDS:
dig, kid

The **kid** likes to sit and **dig**.

The **kid** can **dig** a pit in the sand.

Wow! The pit that the kid digs is big.

Can I sit and dig with you, kid?

Yes! The **kid** lets me **dig** with him.

I can **dig** a pit with the **kid**. It is fun!

Activity Time

Read the words. Then trace the words.

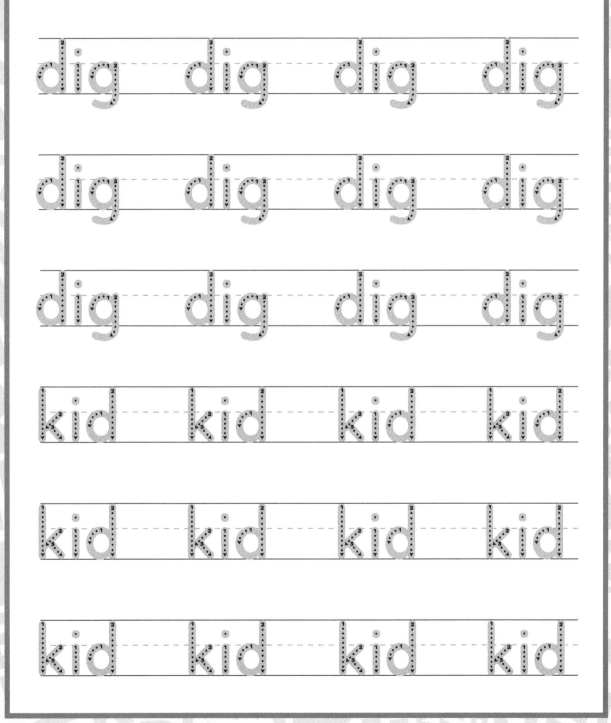

dig dig dig dig

dig dig dig dig

dig dig dig dig

kid kid kid kid

kid kid kid kid

kid kid kid kid

Draw a line from each CVC word to the correct picture.

kid

dig

sit

The Garden

FOCUS CVC WORDS:
got, van

I got out of the van.

I got a big pot out of the van.

I **got** seeds out of the van.

I **got** a jug out of the van.

I got a bag of dirt out of the van.

I got to plant seeds by the van.

LEARN TO READ: CVC WORDS STORYBOOK

Activity Time

Read the words. Then trace the words.

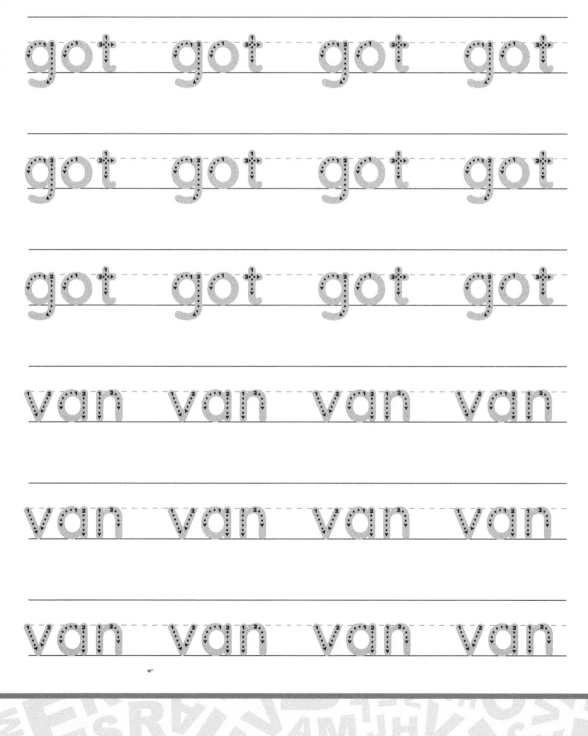

got got got got

got got got got

got got got got

van van van van

van van van van

van van van van

Activity Time

Color the flowers that say **got** or **van**.

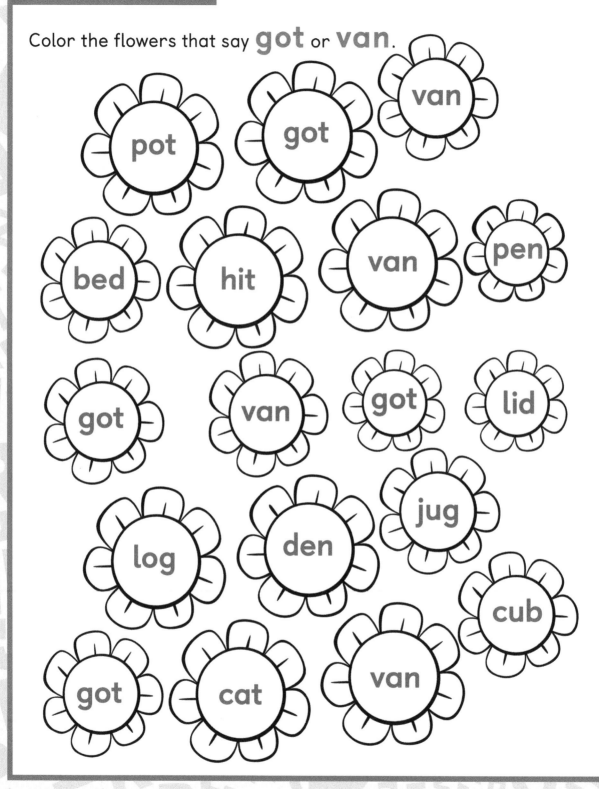

pot

got

van

bed

hit

van

pen

got

van

got

lid

log

den

jug

cub

got

cat

van

LEARN TO READ: CVC WORDS STORYBOOK

Bugs in a Jug

FOCUS CVC WORDS:
bug, jug

The big red bug is in the jug.

The big red bug in the jug has spots.

A big green bug is now in the jug.

Can you see the big bugs in the jug?

Oh! The big green bug flew out of the jug.

The big red and green bugs from the jug are fast!

Activity Time

Read the words. Then trace the words.

bug bug bug bug

bug bug bug bug

bug bug bug bug

jug jug jug jug

jug jug jug jug

jug jug jug jug

Activity Time

Write the words **bug** and **jug** on the lines below.

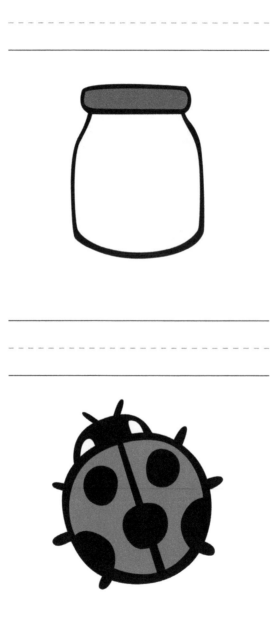

LEARN TO READ: CVC WORDS STORYBOOK

Bath Time

FOCUS CVC WORDS:
cup, tub

I can play in the tub.

Mom put a cup in the tub.

LEARN TO READ: CVC WORDS STORYBOOK

I can fill the cup with
water from the tub.

Dad put a toy in the tub.

The toy in my cup got wet.

A cup and toy in the tub can be fun!

Activity Time

Read the words. Then trace the words.

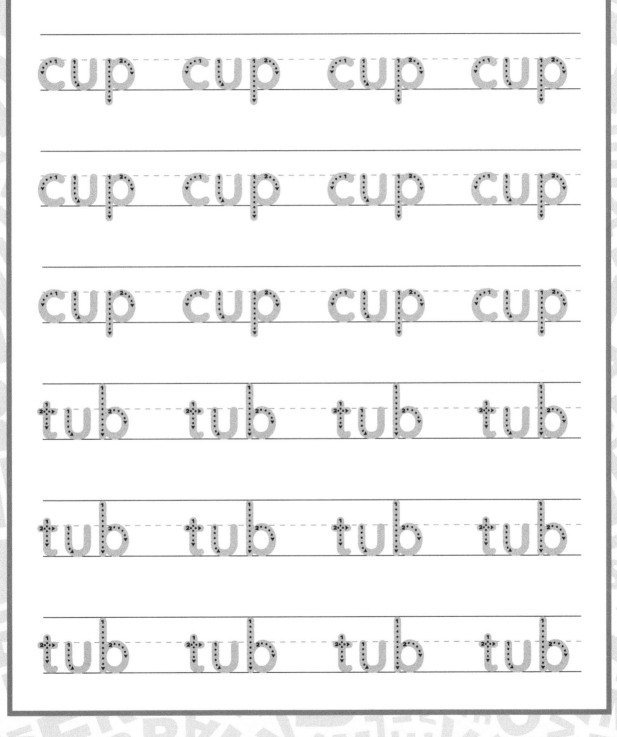

cup cup cup cup

cup cup cup cup

cup cup cup cup

tub tub tub tub

tub tub tub tub

tub tub tub tub

Circle the correct CVC word.

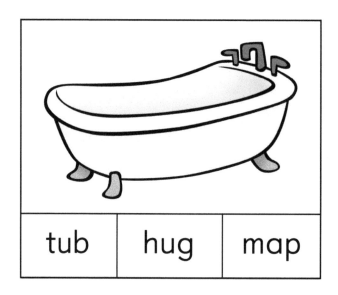

tub	hug	map

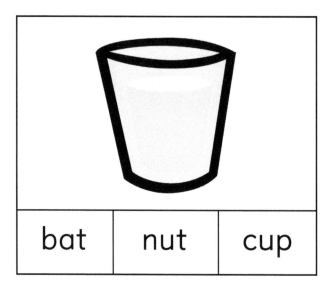

bat	nut	cup

The Park

FOCUS CVC WORDS:
red, ten

I can see ten red flowers.

I can see ten red trees.

I can see ten red bugs.

Oh look, my pal has a red cap, too.

My pal with the red cap
sees ten kids.

We can have fun and
play with ten kids.

LEARN TO READ: CVC WORDS STORYBOOK

Activity Time

Read the words. Then trace the words.

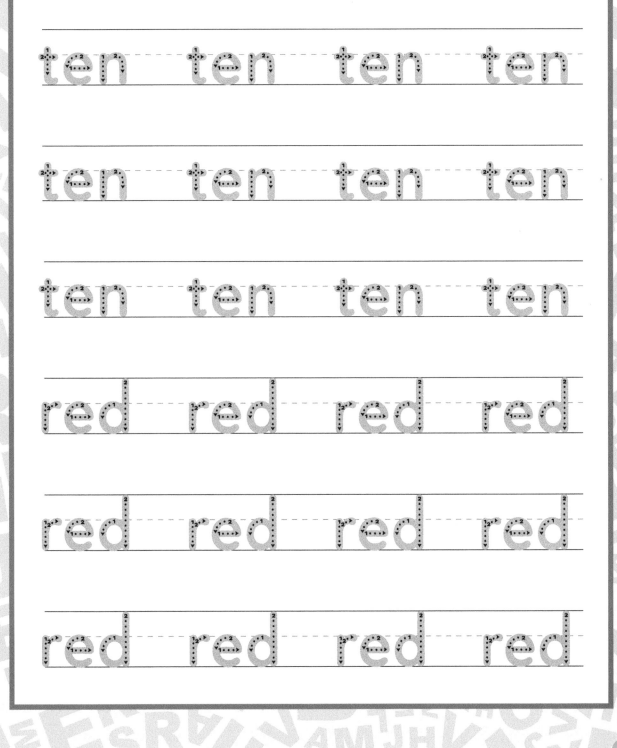

Activity Time

Find the word **red**. Draw a line under each one. Then find the word **ten**. Circle each one.

log

red

sit

red

ten

ten

sun

vet

sun

dad

run

cub

den

run

man

pet

ten

red

sad

mud

vet

ten

dad

vet

bet

Index of CVC Words

INDEX OF CVC WORDS